Sustainable
A green gospel for the age of climate change

Nicola L. Bull &
Mark McAllister

Foreword by
Steve Chalke

First published in Great Britain in 2014 by Nicola L. Bull

Copyright © Nicola L. Bull and Mark McAllister 2014

The right of Nicola L. Bull and Mark McAllister
to be identified as the Authors of the Work has been
asserted by them in accordance with the Copyright, Designs and Patents Act 1988.

Scripture quotations taken from The Holy Bible,
New International Version
Copyright © 1979, 1984, 2011 Biblica, Inc.
Used by permission of Hodder & Stoughton Publishers, an Hachette UK company
All rights reserved.
'NIV' is a registered trademark of Biblica, Inc.
UK trademark no. 1448790

All rights reserved.
No part of this publication may be reproduced, stored
in a retrieval system, or transmitted, in any form or by any means without
the prior written permission of the publisher, nor be otherwise circulated
in any form of binding or cover other than that in which it is published and
without a similar condition being imposed on the subsequent purchaser.

ISBN: 978-1-291-90020-0

*For Ruth, Steve, Judith and Mike
and Sarah, Martha, Ruth and Lydia*

Contents

Acknowledgements	vii
Foreword	ix
Introduction	1
1. Creation and Stewardship	5
2. Covenant	10
3. Sabbath and Jubilee	14
4. Love of Neighbour	19
5. The Work of Christ	24
6. Hope for the Future	28
Endnote	32
Appendix I – Climate Science: an outline of the basic science of human-induced climate change	33
Appendix II – Study Material	45
Further Reading	57
About the Authors	59

Acknowledgements

The material in the six chapters of this book has been drawn from two main sources. While completing a degree in 'Bible and the Contemporary World' at the University of St Andrews during 2011, I researched and wrote about 'Christian Responses to the Challenges of Peak Oil and Climate Change'.[1] My thanks go to Revd Dr Ian Bradley, my supervisor, for his encouragement and advice, and to my fellow students, who have acted as a sounding board for plans for this book.

Particular thanks must also go to the ministers, past and present, of my home church – High Street Baptist Church, Tring, Hertfordshire – who have listened to and supported a range of 'green' initiatives in recent years, with the result that the church was an early collaborator with the town's Transition group, has been awarded Eco-Congregation status twice and has a small but committed 'Green Group'.

Special thanks are owed to Mark McAllister, a former member of the congregation in Tring, whose move to Oasis, Waterloo was the catalyst for the series of church services that provided the second source of material. A request from Steve Chalke – senior minister at Oasis Church – for some sermons looking at sustainability led to an invitation from Mark that I might collaborate with him on this project. For this invitation, Mark's planning and organisation, the warm welcome at Oasis, and Steve's commitment to the series and to taking the message of sustainability forward at Oasis – as well as for contributing the foreword to this book – I am extremely grateful.

The Rt Revd Dr David Atkinson generously gave permission for us to reproduce his background paper on the science of climate change, originally written for Operation Noah. In addition, Bible Reading Fellowship (BRF) kindly allowed us to adapt material from

---

[1] Nicola L. Bull, 'Green Gospel: Christian Responses to the Challenges of Peak Oil and Climate Change', St Andrews, 2011 (MLitt dissertation, unpublished).

their *Guidelines* studies and Church House Publishing gave permission for us to include extracts from *Sharing God's Planet*, a 2005 publication subtitled 'a Christian vision for a sustainable future'.

Nicky Bull, July 2014

Foreword

In a world which is increasingly interconnected and globalised, our lifestyles and choices have a tangible impact on our neighbours – both those who live in our local communities as well as those many thousands of miles away. Yet our God-given mandate to care for, protect and manage the wonderful and awe-inspiring creation, of which we are part, remains an all-too-often overlooked aspect of our Christian mission.

Wherever you dip into the Bible, it is clear that rather than calling for a two-way relationship between the Creator and his creatures, Scripture's real vision is for a triangular relationship between the Creator, his creatures and the whole of his creation. *Sustainable Faith* explores and unpacks this 'green thread' which runs throughout the Bible – from the creation stories of Genesis to the re-creation vision of a renewed heaven and earth in the Bible's last book, Revelation.

But, much more than that, in the pages that follow, Nicky Bull provides a challenging resource which will help to shape the church's response to the critical and ever-more-acute environmental challenges facing our global community. At the moment, everybody, it seems, supports, in principle, our responsibility to work to protect the delicate ecosystem of our blue planet. Opposition only surfaces when cleaning up and caring for the environment costs money or creates inconvenience.

When put on the spot by the religious leaders of his day and asked to name the most important commandment, Jesus astounded his audience, 'The most important one is this: "Hear, O Israel: The Lord our God, the Lord is one. Love the Lord your God with all your heart and with all your soul and with all your mind and with all your strength." The second is this: "Love your neighbour as yourself." There is no commandment greater than these' (Mark 12 29-31).

To come even close to loving our neighbours in the way God intended, we have to face up to the colossal impact that we have on our planet and on their lives. Decisions made, often thoughtlessly, on one side of the globe or town increasingly have a devastating effect on communities which are out of sight and out of mind. More often than not, this impact is felt most keenly by the poorest and most vulnerable. If for no other reason than this, it becomes a fundamental Christian duty to enjoy, steward and respect creation.

Nicky Bull's work thoughtfully reinforces a truth which, to date, the church and the majority of humanity has struggled to come to terms with: the way in which we use our planet isn't working. Not only do we live ecologically unsustainable lives, we also shield ourselves from the natural and human consequences of our actions. Her book reminds us that from the very outset, God inextricably linked humanity and creation. The planet was not simply created as a stage upon which we live our lives – we are part of creation, bonded to it and integrated into it seamlessly. 'For dust you are and to dust you will return' God explains in Genesis.

The great physicist, Albert Einstein, expressed it like this: 'A human being is part of the whole called by us universe, a part limited in time and space. We experience ourselves, our thoughts and feelings as something separate from the rest. A kind of optical delusion of consciousness. This delusion is a kind of prison for us, restricting us to our personal desires and to affection for a few persons nearest to us. Our task must be to free ourselves from the prison by widening our circle of compassion to embrace all living creatures and the whole of nature in its beauty ... We shall require a substantially new manner of thinking if mankind is to survive.'

Our responsibility is, and has always been – though we have been slow to see it – to love and respect the planet as well as its inhabitants.

Having explored the material that follows on the pages of this book with Mark McAllister and Nicky at Oasis Church Waterloo in central London, I know that the content is inspiring yet uncomfortable. It forces us to explore the nagging questions that we all have, but seldom confront, about the level of respect we have for our environment. It challenges us to begin to unpick and examine the complex lifestyles we lead and to re-read the Bible with fresh eyes as we reassess our responsibilities.

Ultimately, *Sustainable Faith* leaves us all with a massive challenge: are we taking the Bible seriously when, in in its very first book, following the famous statement that 'God saw all that he had made, and it was very good', humanity is solemnly charged with an ongoing role – the responsibility and joy of acting as its stewards.

Revd Steve Chalke
Founder of Oasis Global

Introduction

Climate change is scarcely out of the news and yet it does not feature quite so regularly in our churches. This is strange when you consider that we talk and pray, Sunday by Sunday, about wars, about tragedies both international and local, and about natural disasters that cause loss of life. We also pray for our national and local politicians and yet still climate change is hardly ever mentioned. This is despite the fact that 'the issues of climate change are arguably the greatest challenge facing the world today',[2] something acknowledged by government ministers and stressed by environmental activists and others. Many also recognise that some natural disasters, particularly flooding and drought, are exacerbated by the human activities that contribute to climate change.[3] Common sense also tells us that we are using up the natural resources of the planet far more quickly than we are able to recycle the materials used in manufacturing. Modern Western lifestyles, with their rampant consumerism, inbuilt obsolescence and a desire to always have the most up-to-date version of material possessions, are inherently unsustainable. So what should we in the churches be doing – what does our faith tell us in this situation?

A duty of loving care towards the planet and all its inhabitants needs to become a central feature of the Christian message in today's church, accompanied by scriptural backing and practical guidance encouraging God's people to be at the forefront of change. Christians need to be adequately equipped to bring a message of creation care and faith-based environmentalism to their communities. We know that it is not only what we say but what we do that has the potential to 'speak' to people about the love of God in Christ. Demonstrating hospitality, loving our neighbours and caring for the poor are central themes in the gospel message but

---

[2] Personal communication, 10 March 2014, from Minister of State, Department of Energy & Climate Change.
[3] For information on the science and other background to this, see Appendix I.

the 'green' gospel for today must also demonstrate our love and care for *all* creation – humanity is part of a delicate web of life, all of which is loved by our Creator God.

That humanity has been destroying the ecological conditions essential for the continued survival of life on earth is a central religious issue for the twenty-first century. While the church has at times condoned an exploitative attitude towards creation, there are now signs of change. However, it is often only a few committed individuals who are trying to bring the message to the wider church that issues such as climate change and resource depletion really are central Christian themes.

Living more simply, re-using and recycling, reducing our consumption of fossil fuels and becoming more thoughtful and cautious consumers may not 'feel' like Christian discipleship but should nevertheless be an integral part of a twenty-first-century Christian life. In a society where any or all of these can be seen as countercultural, explaining such actions also provides opportunities for Christian witness.

The challenges associated with climate change and finite natural resources are daunting but we do not have to act on our own. God will come alongside us to help us as we seek to do his work here on earth and there is a wide range of initiatives that Christians can engage with. Some of these are faith-based, others are secular; some are local, others are national or international – all are demonstrating a concern for the wellbeing of the planet and all its inhabitants and are seeking the good of future generations. As such, they deserve the support and commitment of Christian people who can bring their skills, abilities – and also their faith perspective – to the task of meeting these challenges.

In the brief chapters that follow, you will find a biblical explanation for a 'green gospel' message together with details of some of the initiatives and campaigns that are current in this second decade of the twenty-first century. By the time you read this book there may well be more opportunities available but this selection is based on a series of six evening services put together for the congregation at Oasis, Waterloo between September 2013 and February 2014, entitled 'Sustainable Faith'.[4] It is far from exhaustive – and this applies not just to the environmental initiatives featured here but to the Bible selections as well. As you come to see how a message of creation care runs like a green thread throughout the biblical narrative – from Genesis to Revelation – you will find your reading of Scripture takes on a new dimension. We are part of God's over-arching plan, fellow-workers with him in the current age, and the central messages of love – love for our Creator God and love for our neighbours – of care for the poor and of seeking justice for all will prompt us to seek a greater understanding of how we can engage with the issues surrounding climate change and sustainability.

How you can use this book

Chapters 1 – 6 have been based on the source material used for a series of six evening church services that were held once a month. You could use them, in your church, as the basis of a series of Sunday morning or evening services over six weeks – or you could expand them to look at Stewardship and Jubilee separately as part of an eight-week series. They could be used in house groups or small groups, with a greater emphasis on discussion and working through thoughts and ideas together, or with part of your time devoted to prayer. There will almost certainly be news stories in the media that relate directly to the topic in hand and that you could use to focus your prayers. Or you could use the material for private study, to deepen your understanding of what God's word has to tell us about the world in which we live and to learn about practical action that you may want to get involved with. Appendix II contains study material that could supplement the chapter text for group or individual study and, for those who wish to read around the whole subject, a book list has been included at the end. However you use

---

[4] The talks given at these services are available in the sermon archive on the church's website: http://www.oasischurchwaterloo.org/.

this book, it is our prayer that you will find it challenging and a source of blessing.

Nicky Bull and Mark McAllister
July 2014

Chapter 1
Creation and Stewardship

What the Bible says
The first creation narrative (Genesis 1:1 – 2:3) tells us repeatedly that all creation is good and it is because it is loved by God (John 3:16) that all creation gains its worth. God cares about the environment and this is the first reason for us to do so.[5] God affirms the goodness of 'vegetation' (Genesis 1:12) and of 'living creatures' (Genesis 1:21, 25). The glory of God is reflected in the extravagance and diversity of creation. This diversity is threatened by human greed when we do not respect the world as God's creation. The main thrust of the first creation story is not to explain how creation came into existence but to instil a sense of wonder – not to encourage praise of creation but to invite the reader to worship the Creator. However, this narrative also contains the phrase that has been used by humanity to justify its domination of the natural world, a phrase suggesting perhaps that human beings are the 'high point' of creation. In Genesis 1:26-27 humans are given a divine mandate to 'rule over' all other creatures and are described as being made 'in the image of God'. However, the special nature of humanity is in the relationship with the Creator that God has given us. The focus is not on human beings as the pinnacle of God's creative work but on the Creator whose nature is reflected in creation. On the basis of work by Jewish scholars, Hodson also concludes that 'by creating us in his image, [God] did not give a justification for the desecration of the rest of creation but rather gave us a responsibility for it. This view helpfully preserves a distinction between humans and other creatures within the context of our accountability to God for our care of creation.'[6]

---

[5] Nick Spencer and Robert White, *Christianity, Climate Change and Sustainable Living* (London: SPCK, 2007), pp. 78-80.
[6] Margot Hodson, 'Environmental Christianity: insights from our Jewish heritage', JRI Briefing Papers No. 13, http://www.jri.org.uk/brief/Jewish_Insights.htm, accessed 23 June 2011.

A fundamental connection between humankind and the very substance of the earth is made clear in the second creation story (Genesis 2:4-25), where we read that it is through soil that the forces of life and death work. God made the first human being out of the earth (*adamah*, Genesis 2:7) and, after they had disobeyed God and eaten of the fruit of the tree of the knowledge of good and evil, the first humans were told that they would return to the soil (Genesis 3:19). Without soil, humans and other living organisms could not survive. It is crucially important for life – it is the ultimate source of virtually everything that we eat – and that the land can be harmed by human activity was documented by both Homer and Plato as well as in the Hebrew Bible (for example, Leviticus 25:4-5).

However, for a number of reasons the church has failed to fully recognise the relationship between God and nature. One reason is the influence of Greek ideas that God is impassive – a divine being who cannot be touched by emotion or events and who is completely separate from and uncontaminated by creation. Second is the anthropocentric view that places humanity centre stage with the natural world as a resource to be exploited; in this view, God is the God of history (*historical*) rather than the Lord of all creation (*cosmological*). Then there is the influence of the belief that matter is intrinsically evil and that only the spiritual is of importance. Although officially the church has rejected such a view, it nevertheless lingers in the attitude encountered by many 'green' Christians – that the church should concentrate on 'saving souls' rather than saving the planet. That the health and wholeness of *all* creation (a state of total wellbeing summarised in the biblical narrative by the word *shalom*) should be a goal of the Christian life has not gained full acceptance.

Creation was not a one-off and finished event; it is an ongoing process in which we are called to participate as co-creators with God. In the accounts in Genesis 1 and 2 we find descriptions of creation that link ecology and economy in 'a community of earth, animal, humanity, and God'.[7] So, while Scripture may not directly address the modern issues of climate change or resource depletion it nevertheless gives general pointers about how humanity should relate to the rest of the creation. 'It is not enough to know that our lives depend on other natural organisms and processes. We need to know how to live out our interdependence responsibly.'[8]

Humanity's position with regard to the whole created order should be one of 'relationship' rather than of dominion, domination, exploitation or control. Just as relationship is at the heart of God – the relationship within and between the Trinity – so relationship is at the heart of all that God has created. The Genesis accounts of creation have been used in the past to justify an attitude of domination and exploitation on the part of humankind. At their heart, however, is a command to human creatures to behave responsibility and in loving care towards non-human creatures and the planet that sustains both humans and non-humans alike.

So, there are clear biblical arguments for the stewardship of creation[9]:

- *We must keep the creation as God keeps us.* Humanity's 'earth-keeping' (Genesis 2:15) mirrors God's keeping of humankind (Numbers 6:24-26). Dominion – not domination – is exercised by humanity joining with the Creator in caring for the land.
- *We must be disciples of the last Adam, not the first.* The vocation of humanity is to share in the restoration and reconciliation of all things.
- *We may enjoy, but not destroy, the grace of God's good creation.* In Genesis 1 God blesses the creatures of land and sea with *fruitfulness*. While expected to enjoy creation and to partake of its fruit, humankind may not

---
[7] Norman Wirzba, *The Paradise of God* (Oxford University Press, 2003), p. 24.
[8] Wirzba, *Paradise of God*, pp. 12, 13.
[9] Based on Calvin B. DeWitt, 'Ecology and Ethics: Relation of Religious Belief to Ecological Practice in the Biblical Tradition', *Biodiversity and Conservation* 4 (1995), pp. 838-848.

destroy the fruitfulness upon which creation's fullness depends. While human beings are commanded to increase from their original number (Genesis 1:28), so also are other living creatures (Genesis 1:22). Human fruitfulness must not be accomplished at the expense of the rest of creation.
- *We must seek first the kingdom, not self-interest.* Fulfilment is a consequence of seeking the kingdom (Matthew 6:33). Matthew 6:25-33 makes clear that the priority for humankind is seeking the way of God rather than chasing after material wellbeing or accumulating the fruits of creation.
- *We must seek contentment as our great gain.* There are *limits* on humanity's role within creation. Not even in the very beginning were the first humans content with the 'good' provision that God had created for them in Eden – dissatisfaction is inherent within fallen human nature but God calls us all, like Paul, to learn the secret of being content (Philippians 4:12b).
- *We must not fail to act on what we know is right.* There must be a strong link between belief and action when it comes to stewardship for creation. We must *do* the truth, making God's love for the world evident by our own actions.

Key verses

Repetition is often a pointer to a really important message in any Bible passage. The goodness of God's creation is stressed repeatedly in Genesis 1 and humanity is seen to be just as much a part of creation as everything else that God made but we are distinguished by the fact that God 'breathed life' into us.

- And God saw that it was good. (Genesis 1:12b)
- Then the LORD God formed a man from the dust of the ground ... (Genesis 2:7)

Genesis 1:1 – 2:3 is creation from the top down, while Genesis 2:4-25 is more human-centred. How many people realise that there are *two* creation stories at the beginning of the Bible?

Reflections and actions
Read Leviticus 25:23-24: '... the land is mine and you reside in my land as foreigners and strangers. Throughout the land that you hold as a possession, you must provide for the redemption of the land.'

We are not owners but tenants of the earth and God is such a generous landlord that he has not even required a deposit! However, we now have a choice: are we going to continue to pollute and damage the environment or are we going to find another way?

There are many actions we can take to reduce our carbon footprint and church communities should be encouraged to provide information, education and assistance on reducing energy consumption. Some may be able to install solar panels on church property, make significant improvements to the insulation of vicarages or manses or work together with other groups in their area on community energy generation schemes. While initial costs for some measures can be quite high, measures taken now will save money in the future. If everyone does their bit it can make an impact.

Whether we replace our light-bulbs with low-energy alternatives or engage a consultant organisation such as the Centre for Alternative Technology (CAT) to completely convert our property to make it low-energy, we can *all* do something.

Key thought

> Making one 7 billionth of a difference ... makes all the difference!

Chapter 2
Covenant

What the Bible says

The biblical account of a great flood, sent by God to destroy all of humankind except for one righteous man and his family, is found in Genesis 6:5 – 9:19. However, the story of a great flood is by no means confined to the biblical account. Such stories are found among the legends from almost every region on earth and many are associated with the story of how the world came into existence. From the Native American Navajo to the Miao of China, people all over the world possess ancient stories with similarities to the biblical account of a worldwide flood. It has been estimated that altogether there may be more than 500 such flood legends and one of the best known of these is the *Epic of Gilgamesh*, dating back to around 2150-2000 BCE. Throughout history and across the globe, as people have tried to explain the beginnings of the world and the existence of good and evil, the same basic story has emerged. Nevertheless, and although 'Noah and the ark' is well known as a Bible story told to children from an early age, the story of the flood stands alongside the destruction of entire populations as rather a troublesome feature of the Bible, a story in which God inflicts suffering on virtually the whole of his creation. However, in an age when climate change and its impacts are rarely out of the news the flood story has much to say about the interaction between God, humanity and creation, and a crucial lesson comes in the aftermath of the deluge.

Following the flood, God renews the command of Genesis 1:28 but this time the covenant is not only with humans but with *all* creation (Genesis 9:8-17). Noah represents a new beginning, a second creation. The writer of Genesis relates the wickedness of humanity and God's decision to destroy them, and the flood story highlights a recurring biblical theme: that other creatures also suffer because of human greed and sinfulness. Robert Murray, who has made a particular study of the covenant theme and traces it through the Bible, notes its key components of justice and peace. He suggests that covenant has ecological as well as spiritual relevance to the world today, and demonstrates that both abuse of the earth and exploitation of the poor are against what he calls the' Cosmic Covenant'.[10] Rowan Williams, former Archbishop of Canterbury, has also said that we should not imagine 'that God's covenant means that we have a blank cheque where the created world is concerned … God's promise has immediate and specific implications about how we behave towards all living beings, human and non-human. It is not a recipe for complacency or passivity.'[11]

Covenant played a central role in the history of God's chosen people, the nation of Israel, and the prophets repeatedly challenged them to return to keeping faith with it – warning them when they had forgotten it. In Hosea 2 and Jeremiah 31 the movements of the earth and sun, day and night and the seasons are all linked with God's promise and with his 'covenantal demands for human justice'. Scripture shows that when we fail to keep the covenant, when we fail to 'act justly, and to love mercy and to walk humbly' with our God (Micah 6:8), then nature responds. Israel understood that the earth would react if the nation betrayed its responsibilities under the covenant and that its rebellion would result in an earth that was 'waste and void' (Jeremiah 4:23-26).[12]

As Christians, we are also in a covenant relationship and therefore 'have a responsibility to live with an awareness of blessings or curses for our actions towards God's earth. We are also

---

[10] Graham Harvey, review of Robert Murray, *The Cosmic Covenant: Biblical Themes of Justice, Peace and the Integrity of Creation* (Sheed & Ward, 1992), in *Scottish Journal of Theology* 50 (1997), pp. 123-124.
[11] Rowan Williams, 'The Climate Crisis: A Christian Response', Operation Noah Annual Lecture, Southwark Cathedral, 13 October 2009, http://www.operationnoah.org/node/90, accessed 17 June 2011.
[12] Diane Jacobson, 'Biblical Bases for Eco-Justice Ethics' in Dieter T. Hessel, ed., *Theology for Earth Community: A Field Guide* (Maryknoll, NY: Orbis, 1996), pp. 49-50.

called to speak against others who would misuse God's earth, and warn them of the consequences of their actions.'[13]

Key verses

- 'I now establish my covenant with you and with your descendants after you and with every living creature that was with you – the birds, the livestock and all the wild animals, all those that came out of the ark with you – every living creature on earth.' (Genesis 9:9-10)
- 'In that day I will make a covenant for them with the beasts of the field, the birds in the sky and the creatures that move along the ground.' (Hosea 2:18)

Reflections and actions

A key document for linking our care for creation with the biblical principles that can underpin Christian environmental care is the Ash Wednesday Declaration, produced by Operation Noah in 2012. The work of Operation Noah (ON), an ecumenical Christian charity founded in 2001, is informed by two main imperatives: firstly, encouraging urgent action to reduce carbon emissions; and secondly, transforming lifestyles into simpler, enriching and more sustainable ways of living. ON is:

- informed by the science of climate change, motivated to care for creation by our faith and hope in God, and driven by the desire to transform and enrich our society through radical change in lifestyles and patterns of consumption;
- rational regarding scientific insights, responsible in addressing the long-term consequences of today's actions, and radical about future lifestyles.

---

[13] Hodson, 'Environmental Christianity'.

The Ash Wednesday Declaration, which was endorsed by a number of church leaders, asks the following questions:

- How do we balance our energy and material consumption with the needs of the poorest communities, and of future generations and other species?
- How do we sustain hope in the midst of fear and denial?
- How can we encourage global cooperation, challenge unsustainable economic systems and change our lifestyles?

These questions then prompt a call to the church to take action.[14] As Christians we are all part of the church – how do you respond to this call? Could you support the work of Operation Noah, either as an individual or as a church community?

Key thought

> **God is in a covenant relationship not only with humans but with *all* creation.**

---

[14] This call is drawn directly from the Bible and it is summarised in Appendix II; see p. 47.

Chapter 3
Sabbath and Jubilee

What the Bible says

According to rabbinic literature, creation was not entirely finished on the sixth day because the 'rest', or *shabat*, of God remained uncreated until the seventh day.[15] So although Genesis 2:1-2 tells us that the heavens and earth were finished on the sixth day, God's creative work was finished only on the seventh day. Viewing creation as taking seven days and not six 'we could conclude that God viewed the need for rest as an integral part of creation itself'.[16] According to Jürgen Moltmann then, 'the whole work of creation was performed *for the sake of the sabbath*'.[17] This calls into question the long-held assumption that creation exists primarily for the benefit of humanity. However, not only in the first creation narrative (Genesis 1:28), but also in Psalm 8 (verse 6) it is clear that creation *is* given to humankind. But this gift does not give us the right to unrestricted use of creation. If God's rest, rather than humanity, is understood as the climax of creation then the practical effect of Sabbath observance is to remind us that the creation is never ours but is forever God's. There is therefore a connection between the destruction of creation and the neglect of Sabbath observance. The pain of creation – both human and non-human – is the result of creation gone awry, creation that has not and is not living out its inner truth and meaning. In the Sabbath,

> ... creation finds its fulfillment, goal, and purpose ... We must learn to see that the deterioration of the earth, which consists of the weakening or destruction of the natural conditions that enable habitats and organisms to

---

[15] Wirzba, *Paradise of God*, p. 35.
[16] Hodson, 'Environmental Christianity'.
[17] Jürgen Moltmann, *God in Creation: An Ecological Doctrine of Creation* (London: SCM, 1985), p. 277.

grow and heal themselves, finds its necessary corollary in social deterioration and injustice. Social justice, we might say, goes hand in hand with ecological justice, since both depend on the human identification with and sympathy for the communal conditions that make for a complete life. The prospect of justice, however, depends on the articulation and implementation of a uniquely human identity and vocation that in seeking the well-being of others, human and non-human, discovers joy and peace.[18]

For Israel, the land was at the heart of their identity as the people of God and it was the law of the Sabbath that provided them with the moral principles intended to guide their agricultural and economic life. The prophet Jeremiah identifies Israel's neglect of divine law, but in particular the Sabbath law, as the reason behind Jerusalem's downfall; the nation's exile in Babylon was a punishment for failing to care for the land.[19] Northcott sees a failure of Sabbath observance as linked to the present disordered economy of work and leisure. He suggests that a day set aside for rest and contemplation serves as a reminder that life does not come from our work but from the Creator and from the lifecycles of the cosmos.[20]

Moltmann argues that in Jesus' actions on the Sabbath – in healing the sick and allowing his disciples to 'work' – he was not flouting the Sabbath law but was proclaiming the arrival of the messianic age (cf Luke 4:18). This age brought with it the freedom with regard to the law that had been promised by the prophets: 'Jesus' proclamation of the imminent kingdom makes the whole of life a sabbath feast.'[21] And if the whole of life is indeed a Sabbath feast then by implication the whole of life involves a call to share in

---

[18] Wirzba, *Paradise of God*, p. 7.
[19] Michael S. Northcott, *A Moral Climate: the ethics of global warming* (Darton, Longman & Todd, 2007), p. 10.
[20] Northcott, *Moral Climate*, p. 187.
[21] Moltmann, *God in Creation*, p. 292.

the outworking of all that Sabbath entails in terms of working for justice and peace for all creation.

As with holding to the covenant, many of the prophets linked Sabbath observance with the restoration of the land and with Israel as a people of God. Leviticus 25:1-17 describes the institution of Sabbath and of Jubilee. Jubilee (Leviticus 25:8-55) – providing rest for the land and restitution of land to its original owners – alongside the Sabbath decrees of Exodus 23:10-12 bring together respect for the sovereignty of God, 'care for the earth, concern for the poor, [and] sensitivity to the needs of both wild and farm animals'.[22] Sabbath, then, is a further key biblical principle for any Christian environmental ethic. However, like all peoples since, the Israelites prioritised personal gain over these God-given guidelines and there is considerable doubt about whether a Jubilee year, as described in Leviticus, was ever actually adhered to.

Key verses

Leviticus 25:1-17 provides links with key criticisms levied against politicians in our own day. These criticisms are that their short-term viewpoint fails to address the destruction of the planet or the creation of massive disparities within society and that the needs of the people are being ignored.

The integrity of the land is important to all of us – it is ultimately what global food production depends upon. However, instead of allowing for fallow periods in which the soil can be restored to fertility, modern agriculture instead maintains intensive cropping with the use of fertilisers to compensate for dead land. The Jubilee principles protect the land, break cycles of poverty and avoid the accumulation of wealth in the hands of a small minority. Such principles would make no sense to modern economists, driven as they are by the imperative to increase profits and GDP, but they underlie the practices of farmers and food producers who operated sustainably for many centuries before the industrial age.

---

[22] Sean McDonagh, *The Greening of the Church* (Geoffrey Chapman, 1990), p. 127.

Reflections and actions
The well-known recycling symbol – three green arrows in a triangle – actually stands not for recycling but for 'Reduce : Reuse : Recycle' and while recycling is now commonplace and, through charity shops and so on, reusing is also becoming mainstream, as a society we have failed to apply the first step, which is to *reduce* our consumption. There are some signs that this may be slowly changing, however, with the growth of internet-based organisations that enable people to collaborate by swapping items, sharing skills, letting homes or cars, etc. Connectivity through mobile phones has made this process even easier and pressing environmental concerns are among the drivers behind the movement. People, and especially the young, are recognising that access is better than ownership and that usage trumps possession. If the point of a film is being able to watch it, then if it can be stored on a computer you do not need to own the DVD; similarly, listening to music no longer depends upon owning records or tapes. On average an electric drill will be used by its owner for only 13 minutes (which makes the price per minute very high indeed), so why don't people share them instead of each having their own?

This trend – collaborative consumption – is also being used to match skills with people who need work done in a London-based enterprise called Echo,[23] which works on the basis of time banking, with one hour being equivalent across the system, whether that is an hour's use of an office, an hour's translation work or an hour building furniture. Rather than directly swapping, hours of time ('echoes') can be banked for future use. This trading creates a journey that leads to the establishing of new links between local people and organisations. It also builds trust between strangers and enhances community – reflecting ideas that, far from being new, are rooted in the Bible.

Can you find out whether there are any skill-sharing initiatives in your area? Could your church offer part of its building, when not in

---

[23] www.economyofhours.com.

use, to local groups so that new networks are established and the church is seen as a 'sharing' community?

Key thought

| **Sharing is better than owning.** |

Chapter 4
Love of Neighbour

What the Bible says
Jesus stated that one of the two greatest commandments was to 'love your neighbour as yourself' (Mark 12:31) and made clear that this love encompasses the whole person, not just their spiritual needs (Matthew 25:35-36). Care for our neighbour is a Christian response to the love of God in sending his Son to die for us. Furthermore, in both the Old and the New Testaments there is an emphasis on considering the good of future generations. We are told to 'care for our unborn successors and for the stranger and the foreigner (Leviticus 19:33-34; Jeremiah 22:3; Matthew 25:35-45)'.[24]

The challenges of climate change and resource depletion highlight the fact that all our actions and choices have repercussions for other people, often people completely unknown to us and in other parts of the world. This is especially so in an age of international trade, when much of what we consume has been grown or manufactured overseas. Trade is important for the development of other countries, but it makes no sense at all, and contributes to increasing CO_2 emissions, when things that could easily be grown or made in this country are shipped half way around the world.

What is now clear is that love of our neighbours – all of humankind, as made clear by Jesus' parable of the Good Samaritan (Luke 10:25-37), not just those whom we instinctively care about – cannot be separated from care for the non-human creation. The world is interdependent; humans cannot survive without the healthy ecosystems that support flora and fauna and provide all that is necessary for the flourishing of life.[25]

---

[24] Robert S. White, *Creation in Crisis* (SPCK, 2009), p. 119.
[25] Dave Bookless, *Planetwise: Dare to Care for God's World* (Nottingham: Inter-Varsity Press, 2008), p. 147.

Key verses
In Chapters 1 – 3, we have largely drawn on teaching from the Old Testament but when it comes to love of neighbour we reach the point where key texts come from the New Testament instead (Mark 12:28-34; Matthew 25:31-46; Luke 10:25-37). However, in Mark 12, Jesus has taken teaching from Deuteronomy and Leviticus and repackaged it in a way that really spoke to his questioner. The love of neighbour is a fundamental teaching of *both* Old and New Testaments but what does this love really look like? In the passage from Matthew, Jesus uses repetition because he wants his hearers to remember this message, which is at the heart of the gospel: our love for our neighbour is not restricted to the spiritual – it is very practical and involves meeting both physical and emotional needs. This leads to the further question of who exactly our neighbour is, and in the story of the Good Samaritan from Luke's Gospel, Jesus answers this very clearly. This is a timeless story and could be rewritten for every place and time. Legalism and fulfilling the law are not the way, but instead, in response to the love of God, we are called to a limitless love for those around us; this was a radical teaching. Jesus placed no limits on the definition of neighbour.

Reflections and actions
The main obstacles for people in a local church who want to encourage creation care as a part of church life very often stem from the view that it is nothing to do with the Christian faith. As a result, too few people see it as a priority and in many churches there is so much else taking up time that even if this view has been overcome you may be faced with the question of what can be done in a church context anyway. Helping your church community to see creation care as intimately tied up with loving our neighbour may be a very useful starting point and once there is group of people, however small, who are committed to seeing green issues moved up the church agenda, their first priority is persuading the church leadership that this is important. Even if church leaders cannot personally devote much time, if they are supportive and will let you

get on and do things then you have a great start. Ideally, a supportive minister will integrate – or infiltrate! – creation-care themes into all aspects of the church's worship, in prayers, in songs and in sermons. In addition, it is important to stress that this whole thing is not about changing light-bulbs or encouraging folk to insulate their lofts or walk to church – however good all these things are, and we all need to do them – it is about being Christian disciples and seeking to follow the teaching of Jesus. Also, whatever local or international outreach initiatives the church is involved with are all part of caring for the world that God has made and so a church may already be doing things that are 'creation care' even if they are not recognised as such. Such actions can be celebrated as part of the church taking steps towards a 'greener' discipleship.

There are a number of outside sources of help for churches wanting to do more. A Rocha's Eco-Congregation programme is an ideal way to start[26] – and as any award gained is valid for only three years it also provides an incentive for ongoing monitoring and looking ahead to what more could be achieved. It is an extremely holistic approach, acknowledging that aspects of a church's work such as lunch clubs, toddler groups and coffee mornings are just as much a part of 'environmental care' in its broadest sense, as are tidying up the churchyard or finding a green energy supplier for the church electricity.

The Transition Network can also be very useful for churches.[27] Set up in 2006, the Transition movement has grown from just two groups (Kinsale in Ireland and Totnes in Devon) to over 1,100 initiatives in more than 43 countries across the world in 2013. Working alongside a local Transition initiative can be an extremely good way of connecting with people outside the church and working together for the benefit of the local community. Some churches may be able to use their buildings to host particular projects, for example during national Recycle Week or Creation

---

[26] http://www.ecocongregation.org.
[27] www.transitionnetwork.org; and see Timothy Gorringe and Rosie Beckham, *Transition Movement for Churches* (Canterbury Press, 2013).

Time, or during local food fairs; they might also use their premises for meetings and film shows hosted by a local Transition group. Can you get involved in a local Transition initiative in your community? Or could you get involved with starting one?

Another way in which individual Christians or church groups can get involved is by joining Christian Ecology Link (CEL), which has a very useful website[28] and can send you regular email updates about what is going on in the 'green' Christian world. They also co-ordinate a programme called *ecocell*, which they describe as a journey, or pilgrimage: 'The final destination of this pilgrimage is sustainable living in our personal lives. When we reach it we will be living within the limits of the resources available on Earth, and of the Earth's capacity to absorb our waste products, perhaps our greatest challenge in the 21st century.'

About 45 people have joined the *ecocell* programme since its launch in January 2011 and most of them are still on the journey, some just as 'observer members' receiving the regular emails containing 'thoughts of the week', prayers, or some other communication. But many of them keep to the discipline of recording their CO_2 emissions from domestic energy and travel each month and making an annual estimate of emissions related to their food consumption.

'You can't claim to love your neighbour and pollute the environment on which he depends. You can't claim to love the Creator and abuse the climate of this beautiful, beloved planet. The Spirit that moves among us is the same Spirit that moves in and through all creation.'[29] This is the message behind efforts to demonstrate to the local church and community that creation care is an integral part of gospel discipleship.

So how are your actions impacting the rest of the world and future generations, both positively and negatively? What new actions can you take to better love your neighbour – in your

---

[28] http://www.greenchristian.org.uk.
[29] Brian D. McLaren, *We Make the Road by Walking* (Hodder & Stoughton, 2014), p. 292.

personal lives, as a community and in lobbying government for change?

Key thought

> **Love for our neighbours cannot be separated from care for the rest of creation.**

Chapter 5
The Work of Christ

What the Bible says
Jesus has been related to the whole of God's creation throughout eternity and the New Testament, rather than replacing the Hebrew Bible's theology of creation, rereads it in the light of Christ. It should come as no surprise, therefore, that many New Testament passages make it clear that it was Jesus, the Son, who was active in the very beginning, in creation. In his teaching, too, Jesus provides guidelines that put care for *all* of creation – human and non-human – at the centre of the gospel. Indeed, 'the sermon on the mount gives pretty precise instructions on how to construct an outlook that could lead to an economics of survival'.[30] In Jesus, God is manifest in a way that is not separate from matter, life, human culture and religion but he is intimately involved with all these very human concerns, something that comes out repeatedly in the gospel narrative as Jesus talks with people, meets needs and challenges attitudes. The story of Jesus tells us of a promise of a new, different future for the heavens and the earth and for human beings.

Christ was the Creator of the world as well as its Redeemer and fully rounded biblical teaching should help us to see Jesus as Lord of creation as well as Lord of each individual Christian's life. Sustainability is at the very heart of Jesus' teaching – and is to be central to our own work-life balance.

Most importantly, any study of Jesus' work always comes to the cross, and its meaning is bigger, deeper and richer than we might imagine. It is not just to be reduced to a simple evangelical formulation but opened out so that its wider implications can be appreciated.

---

[30] E. F. Schumacher, *Small is Beautiful* (Abacus, 1991), p. 129.

Key verses
John 1:1-3
- Jesus' work did not begin on the cross, or even at his birth.
- Jesus' work began in the beginning, with his central role in creation.

John 1:14
- God's plan of salvation is not remote but involves sending his Son to live within the created order.
- Our imitation of Jesus must include getting involved with the issues of the world around us.

Matthew 6:25-34
- Jesus teaches a simple lifestyle based on God's goodness and provision.
- Not 'running after these things' involves not only a lack of concern for material goods but also a lack of acquisitiveness.

Colossians 1:15-20
- On the cross Jesus reconciled *all things* to himself.

The cross is the central event in human history and we should not be surprised when its implications are greater than we at first think. It is all utterly relevant and pertinent to our thinking about how we can live a sustainable life and how we should play our part within the whole of creation. The issue of sustainability runs through the entire biblical narrative, 'like Blackpool through a stick of rock'!

Reflections and actions
A Rocha is a Christian nature conservation organisation, and its name comes from the Portuguese for 'the Rock', as its first initiative

was a field study centre in Portugal.[31] A Rocha projects are frequently cross-cultural in character, and share a community emphasis, with an emphasis on science and research, practical conservation and environmental education. They work all over the world and have been involved with a number of projects in the UK. Their focus is on small, locally run projects and on getting communities involved. It is about doing things practically to celebrate and conserve God's wonderful creation. The church often makes the mistake, when talking about what God made and what God loves, of thinking just about people and A Rocha is about changing how we think – recognising that God loves all of his creation.

In a survey of 25 experts who were asked what 50 things will contribute to saving the planet, the second most important was deemed to be 'faith groups getting active'. The challenge for each of us is how we should respond to this – a journey that involves the heart. The key aims are to *get inspired*, *get informed* and *get involved*. As individuals we can *get inspired* by revisiting our theology (thinking more deeply about the biblical principles underlying creation care, including those described in this book) and by reflecting on the natural world. As individuals we can *get informed* by reading more widely about creation care and the issues and perhaps by joining A Rocha or a similar organisation. And we can *get involved* by reviewing our lifestyles.

As churches we can get inspired by learning from others and networking better. We should also get informed about creation care and the issues as congregations or church groups and get involved by reviewing the lifestyle and mission of the church, our community engagement, campaigning activity and worldview. A really good way in which to begin this process is to undertake the Eco-Congregation Church Check-Up (Module 1), which looks at a number of aspects of church life and also encourages the establishing of priorities for action.

---

[31] www.arocha.org.

Key thought

> Jesus reconciled *all things* to himself.

Chapter 6
Hope for the Future

What the Bible says
In this last chapter we also come to the last book of the Bible, having started our exploration of biblical creation care at the very beginning, with Genesis. And we also come full circle.

'The liberation of creation is to happen at the end of history',[32] when full salvation for earth and for all of creation will be attained in the glory of the resurrection. While we can have this hope for the future this does not in any way absolve us from action in the present. We therefore 'ought to care about creation because of its eternal destiny' and because God's plan to reconcile all things to himself (Colossians 1:20) 'really does include all things'.[33] In Romans 8:19-23 Paul describes creation as frustrated and groaning and part of the reason for this lies in humankind's failure to fulfil its 'God-given mandate to care for it as servant kings'.[34] But, as we have seen already, Christ's death does more than bring wholeness for humanity, it also restores creation – he is the Redeemer of the *world*. The wholeness we experience in the present is a firstfruit and part of the guarantee of a new creation set free from decay and from the harm that we have inflicted upon it. We can partner with God as we strive to achieve a balance between God's sovereignty (he is in ultimate control) and human responsibility (the charge given to us to care for all that God has made).

The view we have of the future of the earth determines how we treat it in the present. Some Christians seem to believe that if this earth is destined for destruction and we will get 'a new heaven and a new earth' – a mistaken reading of Revelation – there is no particular need to care for the planet we are living on. However, the phrase 'new heaven and new earth' occurs not only in Revelation

---

[32] Richard Bauckham, *Bible and Ecology* (Darton, Longman & Todd, 2010), p. 99.
[33] Spencer and White, *Christianity, Climate Change and Sustainable Living*, p. 89.
[34] Spencer and White, *Christianity, Climate Change and Sustainable Living*, p. 91.

21:1 but 'in Isaiah 65:17 and Isaiah 66:22, which are part of one main passage about an ideal world in the messianic age'. There, the newness of the heavens and the earth comes from their freedom from corruption and wickedness. Seeing the Old and New Testament passages side by side gives an image of the earth redeemed and renewed, but *not* of 'the earth as a temporary and disposable commodity'.[35] The important role played by the natural world in the new creation is also demonstrated by parallel passages in Ezekiel and Revelation (Ezekiel 47:1-12; Revelation 22:1-2).

Key verses
In Revelation the sustainable faith of the Garden of Eden is restored. The Tree of Life is a powerful symbol of the hope for the future to which we are called; in Genesis it is contrasted with the Tree of the Knowledge of Good and Evil and in Revelation we read that it bears fruit each month and that its leaves are for healing (Revelation 22:2).

Other key verses are Romans 8:18-22 and Isaiah 65:17-25. The message in Romans is that:

- liberation of creation from its *bondage to decay* is part of the good news of Jesus;
- as with our spiritual transformation, this is *progressive but incomplete* until he returns; and
- 'creation … waits for the children of God to be revealed', ie for *us* to step up and play our part. We are required to be in tune with God's care for creation.

What will creation look like on the day of the Lord? No one knows. However, Isaiah 65, as suggested above, reinforces the continuity that exists between the Old and New Testaments and between creation as we know it now and the new creation: the new heavens

---

[35] Hodson, 'Environmental Christianity'.

and new earth of both Isaiah and Revelation contain an element of continuity with the present. They are built on: equality (Isaiah 65:20); justice (v. 22); productive work (v. 23); and peaceful co-existence (v. 25). While the biblical pictures of hope for the future (every man under his own fig tree, etc) may not be literally true, they show us that there will be a continuity with what is currently known.

Reflections and actions
Many of the resources of modern life (fossil fuels, minerals, potable water) are finite and we have caused environmental damage and destruction of ecosystems in our extraction and use of them. Such destruction has worsened with modern giant machinery: 'We used to take the coal out of the mountains but now we take the mountains off the coal.'

Water is crucial for all life and in the picture of the restored creation in Revelation 22 it is the first thing mentioned (verse 1). Despite the efforts of governments and aid agencies over many years the global situation with regard to water is still far from good:

- 900 million people around the world do not have access to safe drinking water;
- 2.5 billion cannot access good sanitation; and
- 5000 children die every day because of dirty water or inadequate sanitation.

Where clean water is easier to access – where rainwater collecting tanks or boreholes are installed – life is changed, especially for children and young people who otherwise have to make daily water collection journeys. More time can be spent on education, on tending food crops and on having fun. Most dramatically, in some places, girls are no longer exposed to the risk of repeated rape when collecting water.

Water really does make a huge difference to life – and although we take it for granted we can get an inkling of how a shortage of water affects everything if we think about surviving on 10 litres a day – for everything (one full toilet flush uses about 9 litres and the average European uses 100 litres per day)! Many people in developing countries exist with 10 litres per day or less. Bottled water is approximately 2000 times the cost of tap water. Think about it! Would you really spend this on anything else? If you did this for a sandwich, you could be paying about £2000 for it!

Following Jesus is about relationship – and our relationship with the environment in a consumerist society is broken. God wants his followers to fix this relationship so we should think about the way we live – to excess – and consider how we can change. Can each one of us make one initial change right now, whether that is taking shorter showers, turning taps off whenever possible or not buying bottled water? Ideally we should also get involved in the issues connected to water shortage, and climate change is one of these. We can act on behalf of those who do not have a voice.[36] 'We should live with our global neighbour in mind; if our relationship with creation is broken our gospel is incomplete.'[37]

Key thought

> **The Bible narrative begins and ends with creation – and with trees!**

---

[36] More information on these issues can be found on the websites of Tearfund, Water Aid and other overseas aid agencies.
[37] Jo Herbert, Tearfund, speaking at Oasis, Waterloo, 6 October 2013.

Endnote

There are now some signs that churches – and especially those in which national leaders have set an example – are making attempts to include creation care and environmentalism within the day-to-day life of their congregations. There has not yet been the 'ecological reformation' of Christianity, as called for by some, and neither does eco-theology so far have a prominent place in the training of clergy and other church workers. However, history suggests that it is often when change comes from the grass roots that a real and lasting difference can be made.

As you come to the end of these chapters, ponder the following questions, and think about how you might bring your thoughts to a wider group.

How can our understanding of our eternal future lead us to a lack of concern for the earth? Can we imagine a sustainable future for humankind and the earth? What does it look like? What should be our first priorities for achieving it? What role can we and our community play?

If you have been reading alone then perhaps you could suggest a house group meeting to consider sustainability. If your group has studied together then perhaps you could lead a church service introducing these issues to your whole congregation. And if your church has run a series of services based on this material, what are your next steps as a Christian community?

Key thought

> Each of us has the responsibility to live well with what we have been given in terms of our circumstances: where we are, our income, what we are physically able to do. Within these constraints we are *all* called to live lightly on the earth.

Appendix I

Climate Science: an outline of the basic science of human-induced climate change
Dr David Atkinson

The Cavendish Laboratory for Experimental Physics was opened on 16th June 1874, with James Clerk Maxwell, a devout Christian, as its first professor. The Latin inscription on the doors used a quotation from Psalm 111:2, *'Great are the works of the Lord; studied by all who delight in them.'*

Science is crucial to an informed faith; Christian faith gives a firm motivation for scientific exploration.

Climate science has to be seen in its context as one perspective on the world, a vitally important one, but not all that can or needs to be said. From a Christian perspective, science is a way of understanding what we can of God's creation, through using experimental methods and drawing inferences from these to the best explanations we can find. It does not address the wider context of the meaning, purpose, values and responsibilities that we have as human beings in caring for God's world, and expressing love to our neighbours and justice in our human affairs.

Climates are neither good nor bad, but there are good ways and bad ways of managing climate risks and resources. Climate risks tend to affect the poorest communities, in a very unequal world, and we should seek to reduce the number of people who are vulnerable to those risks, and work for fair adaptation. The demand for increasing energy, with its current dependence on fossil fuels, is not sustainable. In order to work for a more just world we need to find new non-carbon based energy resources. Science does not answer the moral – indeed spiritual – questions. But it helps us understand the issues with which we need to deal.

Isn't climate science uncertain?
Yes, in the sense that all science and all knowledge is provisional and open to correction. But it is certain enough. Scientists, like all human beings, sometimes get things wrong and make mistakes. However, we usually operate on the basis that what we 'know' is sufficiently certain for us to make decisions and take actions.

Climate science is particularly open to revision and correction as new information is collected and future models are refined, because of variables such as unpredictable solar activity and interactions within the ocean-atmosphere-ice system. It is a subject of enormous complexity. It is also unclear what feedbacks may occur should average global temperatures rise over a certain level, injecting a further unpredictable element into the science.

So we expect knowledge to be partial and different models to produce different predictions. We are dealing with uncertainties. But there is an overwhelming consensus from climate scientists that we know enough to make policy decisions to move away from dependence on fossil fuels – and that we need to do so urgently. In fact, alongside all uncertainties, there are two clear conclusions: first, that there is increasing scientific confidence in the best climate models to do a very good job; and second, that scientists are increasingly able to identify many more positive than negative feedbacks in the climate system as greenhouse gases accumulate, which lends increasing weight to the case for precautionary action.

Historical background
In the mid-nineteenth century people realised that the climate had changed over time, causing huge events such as ice ages and warm periods in between. Jean-Baptiste Fourier was the first to posit that different gases in the atmosphere absorbed different amounts of radiation. In 1859 John Tyndall first established that molecules of water vapour, carbon dioxide (CO_2), methane, nitrous oxide and ozone (later called 'greenhouse gases') had absorbed 'heat' radiation and hence maintained the surface warmer than would

otherwise be the case, and that therefore changes in 'greenhouse gas' concentrations could have caused changes in the climate.

In 1895, the Swedish scientist Svante Arrhenius argued that halving or doubling the concentration of CO_2 in the atmosphere could lead to changes in the average surface air temperature of the Earth of between 4 and 5°C (degrees Celsius). (Later shown to be more likely to be between 1.5 and 4.5°C.)

Guy Callender was the first (in 1938) to posit an empirical link between the rising concentration of CO_2 in the atmosphere and increase in world temperatures.

There was growing scientific concern in the 1980s, and in 1988 Prime Minister Margaret Thatcher recognised the challenge – which led to a surge of new work and evidence. The monitoring of CO_2 in the atmosphere was started in 1957 at Mauna Loa Observatory, a volcanic mountain on Hawaii, and updated regularly. It shows a steady overall increase from 1957 to the present day in the atmospheric concentration of CO_2.

Scientific collaboration

In 1988 an Intergovernmental Panel on Climate Change (IPCC) was assembled, soon to be mandated by the United Nations. Their First Assessment Report in 1990 broadly confirmed Callender's view. The Second Assessment Report in 1996 said that there is a 'discernible human influence on global climate'. The Third Assessment Report in 2001 (IPCC AR3) concluded that 'most of the observed warming over the last fifty years is likely to have been due to the increase in greenhouse gas emissions'. By 2007, the scientists had become more certain: 'Most of the observed increase in global average temperatures since the mid-twentieth century is very likely (greater than 90% confidence) due to the observed increase in anthropogenic (caused by human activity) greenhouse gas concentrations' (IPCC AR4).

Carbon dioxide levels

The whole period of human civilisation has benefited from a relatively stable global climate (even though regional climates have changed quite markedly during this time).

Atmospheric gases trapped in ice cores from the Antarctic and Greenland show a very rapid increase in the percentage of CO_2 in the atmosphere since the industrial revolution, and especially in the last 50 years. Levels are now 40% above pre-industrial levels. Isotopic analysis indicates that this increase is largely due to the burning of fossil fuels. CO_2 in the atmosphere acts as a blanket over the Earth's surface and together with other 'greenhouse gases' keeps the Earth's temperature about 20 to 30°C warmer than it would otherwise be. Without some CO_2 in the atmosphere we would have extreme cold like Mars, and life as we know it would be impossible.

Of course, there have been significant atmospheric changes over geological time scales, but the concentration of CO_2 has ranged between 180 parts per million (ppm) during ice ages and 280ppm during the brief warm interglacial periods for at least the last 600,000 years until about 1750, when it started to rise further. In 2013 the CO_2 concentration reached 400ppm and it is rising steadily at about 2ppm per year.

The UK Climate Change Act of 2008 says: 'It is the duty of the Secretary of State to ensure that the net UK carbon account for the year 2050 is at least 80% lower than the 1990 baseline.' The later international agreement of the Copenhagen Accord (2009) – a non-binding accord drawn up by the US together with Brazil, India, China and South Africa – includes this:

> The Accord, to prevent dangerous anthropogenic interference with the climate system (http://en.wikipedia.org/wiki/Avoiding_dangerous_climate_change), recognizes 'the scientific view that the increase in global temperature should be below 2°C', in a context of sustainable development

(http://en.wikipedia.org/wiki/Sustainable_development), to combat climate change.

Many governments have adopted (for policy or rhetorical purposes) 2°C of warming as the temperature beyond which climate change becomes 'dangerous' according to UNFCCC.

'Even 2 degrees Celsius is too high'
In a paper published in December 2013, James Hansen and seventeen other climate scientists argued that even the present international goal of limiting carbon emissions to give an odds-on chance of keeping global warming to a maximum of 2°C higher than mid-nineteenth century average *'would have consequences that can be described as disastrous.'* The goal, they claimed, should be to contain further warming to around 1°C (the world is already 0.8°C warmer than the nineteenth century):

> Continuation of high fossil fuel emissions, given current knowledge of the consequences, would be an act of extraordinary witting intergenerational injustice.

What might happen?
If the average surface temperature of the Earth were to rise in the next half century another 2°C beyond today's temperature, it is expected that by and large wet areas will become wetter, and dry areas drier, so there would be more flooding in some areas, more drought in other areas, shortages of drinking water, change in crop yields affecting food security, sea level rise, and health affected through changes in insect distribution and in a variety of other ways.

If the rise were more than 4°C, it is very possible that these effects would be dramatically worsened.

As Sir John Houghton notes, the global temperature difference between the middle of an ice age and the warm periods in between is only about 5-6°C. So, 'likely warming in the 21st century will be a rate of climate change equivalent to, say, half an ice age in less than 100 years – a larger rate of change than for at least 10,000 years. Adapting to this will be difficult for both humans and many ecosystems.'

Christian responses to climate change need to address many aspects of mitigation of the worst effects of climate change, among them severely reducing our dependence on fossil fuels, and also the need for humanity to find ways of adapting to the inevitable changes. Human beings have always had to adapt to changing conditions, and adaptation is happening in many ways all the time. Christian commitment to justice will seek to ensure that the adaptation necessitated by climate change – which can be enhanced with appropriate effort – is as fair as possible, particularly for the most disadvantaged parts of the world.

IPCC AR5 (2013–14)
The Fifth Assessment Report group (IPCC AR5) published its scientific findings in September 2013 and from this the following is clear:

- Warming of the climate system is unequivocal and, since the 1950s, many of the observed climate changes are unprecedented over decades to millennia. The atmosphere and ocean have warmed, the amounts of snow and ice have diminished, sea-level has risen and the concentrations of greenhouse gases have increased.
- Each of the last three decades has been successively warmer at the earth's surface than any preceding decade since 1850. In the northern hemisphere, 1983–2012 was probably the warmest 30-year period of the last 1400 years.
- The slight slowing in the rate of surface warming over the 15 year period 1998–2012 compared with the rate over the past 50 years, does 'not reflect long term trends'.

- Ocean warming dominates the increase in energy stored in the climate system, accounting for more than 90% of the energy accumulated between 1971 and 2012.
- Over the last two decades, the Greenland and Antarctic ice sheets have been losing mass, glaciers have continued to shrink worldwide, and Arctic sea ice and northern hemisphere spring snow cover have continued to decrease in extent (although Antarctic sea ice has been increasing).
- The atmospheric concentrations of CO_2, methane and nitrous oxide have increased to levels unprecedented in at least the last 800,000 years. CO_2 concentrations have increased by 40% since pre-industrial times, primarily from fossil fuel emissions and secondarily from emissions arising from net land use change. The ocean has absorbed about 30% of the emitted anthropogenic CO_2, causing ocean acidification (which affects fish stocks).
- Human influence on the climate system is clear. It is extremely likely that human influence has been the dominant cause of the observed warming since the mid-twentieth century.
- Limiting climate change will require substantial and sustained reductions in greenhouse gas emissions.
- Global surface temperature change for the end of the twenty-first century is likely to exceed 1.5°C relative to 1850–1900 [for almost all the emissions pathways and climate models]; 0.8°C warming has already occurred. Relative to the average from 1850 to 1900, global surface temperature change by the end of the twenty-first century is projected probably to exceed 1.5°C but unlikely to exceed 4°C.
- It is virtually certain that there will be more frequent hot and fewer cold temperature extremes. The global ocean will continue to warm. It is very likely that the Arctic sea ice cover will continue to shrink, and glacier volume

further decrease. Global mean sea level will continue to rise.

The Fifth Assessment Report group has since published the second part of its Report, 'Impacts, Adaptation and Vulnerability' (IPCC AR5.2, March 2014). This new report refers to the risks that climate change brings of different impacts in different parts of the world. In summary, these are:

- risk of death, injury or ill-health or disrupted livelihoods in low-lying coastal zones and small islands due to storm surges, coastal flooding and sea-level rise;
- risk of severe ill health and disrupted livelihoods for large urban populations due to inland flooding;
- systemic risks (breakdown of infrastructure and critical services such as electricity, water supply, and health and emergency services) due to extreme weather events;
- risks of mortality and morbidity during periods of extreme heat;
- risks of food insecurity (negative impact on yields of maize and wheat), and the breakdown of food systems;
- risk of loss of rural livelihoods and income due to insufficient access to drinking water and irrigation water and reduced agricultural productivity;
- risk of loss of marine and coastal ecosystems, biodiversity and the good they provide (especially for coastal livelihoods, fishing communities in the tropics and in the Arctic);
- risk of further ocean acidification which will affect fish stocks and the whole marine ecosystem;
- risk of loss of terrestrial and inland water ecosystems and biodiversity;
- risk of social unrest and conflict through uncertainty about food security and more competition for resources; and

- heightened likelihood of people being displaced from their homes.

The report also underlines the fact that it is people living in poverty 'who are socially, economically, culturally, politically, institutionally or otherwise marginalised' who are especially vulnerable to climate change. Changes in migration patterns are noted and while few extinctions of species have been attributed yet to climate change, the report notes that much slower rates of climate change during the past millions of years have nevertheless caused 'significant ecosystem shifts and species extinctions'.

The authors also refer to what they call 'large scale singular events'. With increased warming, some physical systems or ecosystems may be at risk of abrupt and irreversible changes ('tipping points'). The risks increase disproportionately as temperature increases. Some risks are low, but under high-emissions scenarios they could be catastrophic.

The third part of the IPCC Fifth Assessment Report (IPCC AR5 Working Group 3), 'Mitigation of Climate Change', was published in April 2014, and assesses all relevant options for mitigating climate change through limiting or preventing greenhouse gas emissions, and enhancing activities that remove them from the atmosphere. It discusses the various implications of different options, but does not specifically recommend any one particular approach.

UK Committee on Climate Change Review (2013)
The Fourth Carbon Budget Review of the UK Committee on Climate Change, which advises the UK government, was published in November 2013. It largely endorses IPCC AR5, though says rather more definitely that in a scenario where global greenhouse gases continue to increase, 'it is likely that global temperature will

increase by 4°C or more above pre-industrial levels by the end of the century.' They argue that:

- Scientific evidence now shows even more clearly that human activity is heating the earth.
- Globally, ocean heat content is increasing, glacial ice, Arctic sea ice and snow are retreating, sea level and surface temperatures are rising.
- Tentative estimates are now available for feedbacks in the climate system. One such feedback with potentially significant warming is carbon release from melting permafrost. The net effect of these newly quantified feedbacks is likely to be further warming above that projected by current models.
- Current evidence continues to point towards major risks to human welfare and ecological systems over the twenty-first century as a result of human-induced climate change. These risks can be limited by taking global action to reduce greenhouse gas emissions.
- It is worth adding to the last sentence that the Christian call to justice in meeting human development needs, increasing our human capacities for adaptation, and the availability of new technologies etc., can all help minimise such risks.

The urgency for a change of course is growing
Most aspects of climate change will persist for many centuries even if emissions of CO_2 are stopped now. However, substantial and sustained reductions in greenhouse gas emissions will slow down and reduce (but not eliminate) the magnitude of the changes in climate that will occur.

Some scientists speak about 'tipping points' (see above), where some element in a complex system can change more rapidly than the forcing which is applied to it. The element may not then return to its original value. The element in the system moves to a different state. For example, Arctic sea ice is melting fast. The rapid decline that has been observed in the last two decades has been surprising. Predictions about the future are extrapolated from recent observations. Would the ice re-form if the temperature dropped again? No one knows. Ice reflects radiation back into the atmosphere, so would further ice loss mean that global warming is significantly increased? Many scientists think this so-called ice-albedo effect is very likely.

There are huge amounts of carbon locked up in permafrost, which is melting rapidly, though recent work indicates that warmer Arctic ecosystems could act as a powerful sink for such CO_2 released. There are huge amounts of methane hydrates in a solid state at the bottom of deep oceans. Methane is far more effective in promoting global warming than CO_2 and if the oceans heat up, will the methane be released as a greenhouse gas into the atmosphere?

Very recent research in New South Wales, on cloud formation that could well affect global temperature, raises further questions that scientists are addressing and offers conclusions that need to be verified.

Having reviewed various technological and economic options for mitigating and adapting to anthropogenic climate change, Professor James Hansen, formerly climate scientist at NASA, wrote:

> The basic matter, however, is not one of economics. It is a matter of morality – a matter of intergenerational justice. The blame, if we fail to stand up and demand a change of course, will fall on us, the current generation of adults. Our parents honestly did not know that their actions could harm future generations. We, the current generation, can only pretend that we did not know.

Christians agree. As The Ash Wednesday Declaration[38] 'Climate Change and the Purposes of God', referring to our God-given responsibility to care for God's Earth, put it:

> Whereas previous generations did not know the damage they were causing, we do. We must use our power wisely to promote the flourishing of future generations and the diversity of life on earth. This is the responsibility of every church and every believer … To seek justice for all, for present and future generations, our authorities must encourage and enable all people to live fairly and sustainably. Acting justly requires us to hold our governments and corporations to account.

This has been endorsed by senior church leaders, for example:

> If ever there were an urgent moral and spiritual issue, this is it. We risk a twofold betrayal – of our responsibility to the Creator for the good stewardship of His creation, and of our responsibility to our vulnerable neighbours, here and worldwide, who bear the brunt of environmental degradation and looming crisis – not to mention our responsibility to generations to come, our own children and grandchildren. We need to show a deeper faithfulness to God and our neighbour, and this campaign calls us to do just that.
> (Dr Rowan Williams, Former Archbishop of Canterbury, in the CofE Diocesan Environment Officers' campaign leaflet, *Hope for the Future*)

---

[38] Published by Operation Noah in February 2012; see http://www.operationnoah.org/ash-wednesday-declaration.

Appendix II

Study Material

1. <u>Creation and Stewardship</u>

A good creation[39] (Genesis 1:1-25)
The opening words of Genesis are majestic. The writer declares that God is before everything and that he created everything. Whatever the mechanism of creation, Genesis declares that it has its origins in a Creator God.

The word 'good' is used seven times in this chapter (seven being a symbol of perfection). God's creation is good – every bit of it. At different times in history, there have been debates over the goodness of the world and this thinking has led to a devaluing of our natural world. Yet the biblical text challenges this view. The material world is made by God, and he saw it as good before humans were created. The value God places on each part of creation is shown by the careful way in which the different aspects of the cosmos and our own planet are described.

- If each part of creation has value in its own right, should we not approach it with the view that it belongs to God and not to us?

Humans and nature[40] (Genesis 1:26-30)
At the end of Genesis 1, we see the creation of humans as the last stage of God's good creation. Humans are commanded to be fruitful and fill the earth (v. 28).

---

[39] Based on Margot Hodson, *Guidelines* (Bible Reading Fellowship, Jan-April 2013) p. 3. See http://www.biblereadingnotes.org.uk.
[40] Based on Margot Hodson, *Guidelines* (Bible Reading Fellowship, Jan-April 2013) p. 4.

The command to 'subdue' the earth (v. 28) has been highlighted by those seeking to challenge the positive concept of biblical stewardship. The Hebrew word (*kabash*) literally means to 'tread down', but it is usually used to describe ploughing. Placed together with a command to reproduce, it provides a picture of humans farming the land to produce food for a growing family. We need to place this teaching alongside our study of Genesis 1:1-25. There should be a balance between adapting ecosystems for our own use and safeguarding nature because we recognise that it has value in its own right. How we can manage the balance of that relationship is explained as the biblical teaching on the environment unfolds.

The Hebrew word for 'rule' (*radah*) is a key concept in verse 28 (NIV), but it is also controversial. The NRSV follows the King James Bible, translating it as 'dominion', which might imply an exploitative rule over the natural world. However, we detect a different meaning once we know that the same word is used to describe Solomon's God-given rule over Israel (1 Kings 4:24). To 'rule', in biblical thinking, means to be given a responsibility. The rule of humankind should be life-giving rather than exploitative.

- How well have we exercised leadership over the rest of creation, given to humanity as our very first responsibility?

2. Covenant

In Genesis 9 God entered into a new covenant with all creation. How can we reflect God's desire in this covenant in the way that we relate to creation? A key document that can help us to link our care for creation with the biblical principles that should underpin Christian environmental care is the Ash Wednesday Declaration, produced by Operation Noah in 2012. This was endorsed by a number of church leaders and its key points are summarised below. Questions have been added to prompt further thought and discussion.

The Ash Wednesday Declaration – Climate change and the purposes of God: a call to the Church[41]

- How do we balance our energy and material consumption with the needs of the poorest communities, and of future generations and other species?
- How do we sustain hope in the midst of fear and denial?
- How can we encourage global cooperation, challenge unsustainable economic systems and change our lifestyles?

These fundamental questions prompt this urgent call to the church:

FIND JOY IN CREATION! Everything that we have comes to us as gift. This is the ground of our worship. The beauty and harmony of God's creation is a source of human wellbeing, spiritual nourishment and joy.

- Do we think of creation primarily as gift – or do we treat it as a resource, from which we take what we want without enough thought for its conservation and protection?
- Do you support any of the nature conservation charities, and if so do you see this as part of your Christian care for God's gift?

LISTEN! In recent decades climate scientists have warned of the dangers of catastrophic climate change resulting from human activity. Instability in weather systems is already bringing destruction and suffering to millions of people. Climate change could result in the loss of livelihoods or of life and the extinction of countless species. This matters because the wellbeing of all creation matters to God (Psalm 145:9). Prophets are those who speak truth, usually uncomfortable truth, to their generation. We must listen to

---

[41] For a five-session study course based on the Ash Wednesday declaration – ideal for church or home groups – see http://www.operationnoah.org/node/529.

the scientists warning us of approaching dangers, exercise discernment and be wary of 'false prophets' representing the vested interests of the powerful.

- Think about prophets in the church today. Would you include those who speak out about climate change, injustice, poverty or how we spend our money?

REPENT! Continuing to pollute the atmosphere when we know the dangers, goes against what we know of God's ways and God's will. We are failing to love not only the earth, but our neighbours and ourselves, who are made in God's image. God grieves over the destruction of creation and so should we. Repentance means finding creative, constructive and immediate ways of addressing the danger.

- Can you see parallels between the picture of the world given in Genesis 6:1-8 and some aspects of twenty-first-century living?
- Do you know of examples of parts of the world where the land, animals or plants are being damaged by the actions of human beings?

TAKE RESPONSIBILITY! Humans have unique responsibility for the wellbeing of creation. We are to care for the earth because it is gift, the product of God's love. Humanity has always had the capacity to destroy our environment, but today we have this to an unprecedented extent. We must use our power wisely to promote the flourishing of future generations and the diversity of life on earth. This is the responsibility of every church and every believer.

- Does your church acknowledge openly that it has a responsibility towards future generations and that it should care for the diversity of all life?
- If not, why not?

SEEK JUSTICE! God is just and requires justice in response from us. This justice applies to poor communities already suffering the devastating consequences of climate change, to future generations, and to all other creatures. Today, the challenge is to seek a different, sustainable economy, based on the values of human flourishing and the wellbeing of all creation, not on the assumption of unlimited economic growth, on overconsumption, exploitative interest and debt.

- Would you consider getting involved with an organisation that works for justice or that is looking at alternatives to current economic models designed around continuing growth and profit?
- Can you think of passages from the Bible that talk about these issues?

LOVE OUR NEIGHBOURS! Christ teaches us to love all our neighbours, extending to our grandchildren and future generations. Loving our neighbour requires us to reduce our consumption of energy for the sake of Christ, who suffers with those who suffer. To live simply and sustainably contributes significantly to human flourishing.

- Have you ever considered that cutting your energy consumption could be one way of demonstrating love for your neighbour?

ACT WITH HOPE! Hope in God motivates us to take action that can lead to transformation, for by God's power at work within us, God is able to accomplish more than we can ask or imagine. Despite the strong probability of very serious effects from global warming, for Christians despair is not an option. It is when we follow Christ and the way of the Cross, in response to his grace, that we experience the God of hope who gives us joy and peace.

- Look into the work of A Rocha or the Transition Movement and talk about how involvement with their projects can convey a joyful sense of hope and can empower people as they seek to live in a more sustainable way and to celebrate creation.
- Could your church support one or both of these organisations?

3. <u>Sabbath and Jubilee</u>

Called to the land and called to justice[42] (Leviticus 25)
In the opening sentences of Leviticus 25, there are two clear statements about human relationship with the land. First, the land is a gift of God: it belongs to him, not us. Secondly, we are called to respect limits and to have our sabbath rests, not simply each week but one in every seven years. In all of this we are called to be a part of a three-way relationship between God, people and planet. Interestingly, this relationship with the land is not about a respect for nature pointing back to a hunter-gatherer existence. It is clear from this passage and those that we read earlier, in Genesis, that farming is the way in which we are expected to interact with the natural world in our daily lives. We are called to roll our sleeves up and get involved. Biblically, it is OK to make adaptations of natural systems and to live off the fruits of creation, but it is not OK to farm beyond the limits of the land. We must leave the edges of our fields for the poor (Leviticus 19:9-10). The land must have its year of rest, when, presumably, wildlife will also take their share of its bounty (Leviticus 25:7).

If these guidelines are kept, there is a promise that the people will live in safety and have food to eat (Leviticus 25:19). Clearly that is not the case today for many people in parts of the world where famines still occur. Our collective loss of a sense of limits has led to

---

[42] Based on Margot Hodson, *Guidelines* (Bible Reading Fellowship, Jan-April 2013) p. 6.

our changing climate and many other environmental problems. Those suffering the consequences are often not those who have benefited from human overuse of the land. Leviticus 25 provides a basis for a specific relationship to a specific land. Each tribe and family in Israel was given land as a gift from God, for themselves and for their descendants. If they fell into poverty and were forced to sell their land, their family could regain it in the year of jubilee. Today, many of the world's people live in cities, with global networks. We have lost the sense of connection to a specific location. We also need to regain our sense of relationship with our own land – be that rural or urban. In both situations, God gives us land as a gift, and nature as a blessing. He asks that we care for the land in which he places us, including the human elements, such as buildings, as well as the natural environment. Urban areas can seem less connected with nature, and yet it is often the natural elements, such as trees and lawns, that make them attractive.

- Do you feel a sense of connection with your local environment?
- If so, does this extend beyond your garden or allotment to the built environment?
- How does it affect how you feel about solar panels or wind turbines?

4. Love of Neighbour

The following includes material taken from *Sharing God's Planet*, a document commissioned by the Church of England's Mission and Public Affairs Council.[43] Questions have been added to prompt discussion and further study.

---

[43] http://www.churchofengland.org/media/1258771/gs1558.pdf. Used with permission.

Air

The wind blows where it wills, and you hear the sound of it, but you do not know whence it comes or whither it goes; so it is with everyone who is born of the Spirit. (John 3:8)

When you next find yourself walking, feel the air on your face, become aware of your breathing, and realise the total and automatic dependence of the life of your body on the atmosphere. Gain a sense of 'being breathed' rather than the other way around. See how the air is one thing: wind, breath, invisibly supporting, moving and enlivening all things. Become aware that this same atmosphere is warming up and that for some living things, human, animal and plant, the twenty-first century will see the final destruction of their habitats and their livelihoods.

- Do you take clean air for granted?
- How does it make you feel when you see pictures of badly polluted cities, where people regularly wear face masks just to go about their daily business?
- Do your feelings have an impact on how often you use a car or travel by plane?

Water

For I will pour water on the thirsty land, and streams on the dry ground. (Isaiah 44:3)

When you next do something involving water – such as drinking a glass of it, watering a plant, or taking a shower – think about the cycle of water through the universe. Become aware of it travelling to where it is needed, for nourishment, growth or cleansing. Think of the water of baptism, by which you affirm your responsibility to the whole community. Water embodies the possibility of rebirth, empowerment and the hope of a renewed creation. In the rainfall, in rivers and oceans, in watersheds – and in your drinking and your washing – water cleanses, nourishes and heals. Polluted water transforms nourishment into poison. Absence of water kills very quickly, but not quickly enough for the terrible suffering of thirsty people and land. It is estimated that within ten years more than 40% of the world's most vulnerable people will suffer from water shortages.

As with the air we breathe, it is easy to take clean water for granted but for many it is a luxury and has to be used sparingly. We have experienced water shortages in the UK even in years with apparently plentiful rainfall.

- Has your church looked at how much water it uses and at ways to conserve water?
- Have you taken steps to reduce your own use of water at home?

5. The Work of Christ

Jesus was prophet, priest and king. He also called us to follow him, so in thinking about the work of Christ we are challenged about our own role. What, then, is the proper place of humanity on the planet? The Bible offers three roles: **prophets**, **priests** and **kings**.[44]

A **prophet** is one who perceives things as they truly are and who speaks of what they see. In *The Brothers Karamazov*, Starets Zosima says:

> Love all of God's creation, love the whole, and love each grain of sand. Love every leaf, every ray of God's light. Love animals, love plants, love every kind of thing. If you love every kind of thing, then everywhere God's mystery

---
[44] What follows is adapted from *Sharing God's Planet*, http://www.churchofengland.org/media/1258771/gs1558.pdf

will reveal itself to you. Once this has been revealed to you, you will begin to understand it ever more deeply with each passing day. And finally you will be able to love the whole world with an all-encompassing universal love.

Once they see, the prophet must speak. Christ exemplified this. His programme of work, as declared in Luke 4, can be understood in a way that is directly relevant to this theme:

> The spirit of the Lord is upon me, because he has anointed me to preach good news to the poor. He has sent me to proclaim release to the captives and recovering of sight to the blind, to set at liberty those who are oppressed, to proclaim the acceptable year of the Lord.
> (Luke 4.18-19)

It is a prophetic role to speak of the beauty and goodness of the creation, to make people see things as they really are and to free the earth from the oppression of exploitation, ignorance and plunder.

The **priest** is primarily active. Human beings should transform nature with the understanding that it is a gift from God, knowing that once the transformation is effected, the creation must be offered back to God. Christ is the supreme exemplar of the priestly role. As priests, human beings have the choice to live sacramentally, receiving all creation as a gift, transforming it and returning it to God, or to live selfishly, separating creation from its source and accruing it to themselves exclusively.

The third human role is that of **kingship**. The servant-king defends the rights of the poor and disadvantaged. The role to which the first Adam was called and failed to fulfil, the role to which Christ and the children of God that follow him are now called, was to 'till and keep' the garden (Genesis 2.15). This is the kingly role, the exercise of dominion for humanity to fulfil, commanded of Adam before the Fall and prophesied by Isaiah. Dominion is an exercise of vice-regency: lordship under God. The biblical term for humanity's relationship with creation is 'steward'. A steward is a servant who relates to God, on whose behalf they exercise dominion. They are also called to render an account to God of their stewardship of tilling and keeping.

- Christ was prophet, priest and king. We are called, as his disciples, to follow him and to be Christ-like; how can we act prophetically, live sacramentally and be good stewards of creation as we attempt to fulfil these roles in our time?

6. <u>Hope for the Future</u>

Christian hope gives us a vision of God's kingdom as a new creation, a creation healed and in which all is made new. Our task is to care for God's earth so that we contribute to the healing and restoration of the planet that is home to humanity and to all God's creatures.

In the biblical flood story we have seen that there is a dramatic parable for our time. It tells of the devastating consequences possible when human wickedness threatens to dominate the earth and when humanity seeks to blame others rather than admit responsibility. But it also tells of how God can use humanity in a divinely guided project to conserve biodiversity for the future benefit of all creation. So, in the words of the Ash Wednesday Declaration,

> We are called to faith and action in trusting response to the God made known by the Holy Spirit in the life, death and resurrection of Jesus, the Lord of all life. As Christians we can live in hope, despite the dangers that threaten us. Through God we hope for new life for all creation (Romans 8:19-25). Our planet, made new by the meeting of heaven and earth, will have an abiding value in the purpose of God (Revelation 21:1-5). We are called to live

and work with hope in response to God's gift, and in the light of God's future: the promised coming of Christ's reign over all.

The resources of the planet are finite and with a growing world population and increasing industrialisation we are using these resources ever more quickly. However, humanity is skilled at adapting to challenges and in the future there will almost certainly be great advances in science and technology, helping us to re-use and recycle the materials that we need. Nevertheless, if all the people of the world are to have an opportunity to enjoy life at more than a subsistence level many of us will need to learn how to adopt less wasteful and more sustainable lifestyles.

- What have you learned from the Bible and from the initiatives mentioned in this book that can help you to address these issues?
- Are you – and your church community – prepared to respond to the challenge of a 'sustainable faith'?

Further Reading

David Atkinson, *Renewing the Face of the Earth* (Canterbury Press, 2008)

Carla Barnhill, *The Green Bible Devotional* (HarperCollins, 2009)

Richard Bauckham, *Bible and Ecology* (Darton, Longman & Todd, 2010)

Dave Bookless, *Planetwise* (IVP, 2008)

Timothy Gorringe and Rosie Beckham, *Transition Movement for Churches* (Canterbury Press, 2013)

The Green Bible (Collins, 2008)

Martin J. Hodson and Margot R. Hudson, *Cherishing the Earth* (Monarch, 2008)

James Jones, *Jesus and the Earth* (SPCK, 2003)

Sebastian C. H. Kim and Jonathan Draper, eds, *Christianity and the Renewal of Nature* (SPCK, 2011)

Natan Levy et al., *Sharing Eden* (Kube Publishing, 2012)

Sean McDonagh, *The Greening of the Church* Geoffrey Chapman, 1990)

Jürgen Moltmann, *God in Creation: An Ecological Doctrine of Creation* (SCM, 1985)

Michael S. Northcott, *A Moral Climate: the ethics of global warming* (Darton, Longman & Todd, 2007)

Chris Polhill, ***A Heart for Creation*** (Wild Goose Publications, 2010)

Catherine von Ruhland, ***Living with the Planet*** (Lion, 2008)

Colin A. Russell, ***Saving Planet Earth*** (Authentic, 2008)

Nick Spencer and Robert White, ***Christianity, Climate Change and Sustainable Living*** (SPCK, 2007)

Sarah Tillett, ed, ***Caring for Creation*** (BRF, 2005)

Ruth Valerio, ***'L' is for Lifestyle*** (IVP, 2008)

Robert S. White, ***Creation in Crisis*** (SPCK, 2009)

Norman Wirzba, ***The Paradise of God*** (Oxford University Press, 2003)

About the Authors

Nicola (Nicky) Bull has an MA in Biochemistry from Oxford University and MSc and MPhil degrees in Human Nutrition and in Dietary Survey Methodology from London. She has four adult children and after a career in the scientific civil service she changed direction to work in publishing, specialising mainly in Christian books as a freelance copy editor and proof-reader. She has been a member of her local Baptist church for almost 30 years and recently completed an MLitt in Bible and the Contemporary World at St Andrews. She is a member of the Board of Operation Noah and when not involved in environmental activities she researches and writes about family history and knits.

Mark McAllister has worked in the international oil and gas business for over 30 years, following an MA in Engineering from Cambridge University. In 2009, he was awarded an honorary doctorate from Robert Gordons University for services to the oil industry. Mark also has a BA in Theology from the London School of Theology. His thoughts on the relationship between climate change and the oil industry were published as an article in *Faith in Business Quarterly*. When the last of their four daughters left home in 2012, Mark and his wife Jennifer moved to Kennington, where they attend Oasis Waterloo and are great fans of the Boris bikes.

Printed in Great Britain
by Amazon.co.uk, Ltd.,
Marston Gate.